WARS DAY BY DAY

WORLD WAR II

1939–1945

Hermann Black

FRANKLIN WATTS

**This edition first published in 2008
by Franklin Watts**

Franklin Watts
338 Euston Road
London NW1 3BH

Franklin Watts Australia
Level 17/207 Kent Street
Sydney, NSW 2000

© 2008 The Brown Reference Group plc
First Floor, 9-17 St. Albans Place
London N1 ONX

www.brownreference.com

ISBN: 978-0-7496-8415-0

Dewey number: 940.53

Editor: Peter Darman
Children's Publisher: Anne O'Daly
Editorial Director: Lindsey Lowe
Creative Director: Jeni Child
Designer: Reg Cox

Photographic credits:
All photographs U.S. National Archives except the following;
Robert Hunt Library: 6 (both), 8, 10 (bottom), 16 (bottom),
28 (bottom), 29, 33, 38 (bottom), 41, 42 (bottom), 44 (bottom)

Printed in the United States

Franklin Watts is a division of Hachette Children's Books,
an Hachette Livre UK company.
www.hachettelivre.co.uk

Contents

Introduction 4

1919–1938 6

1939 11

1940 15

1941 21

1942 26

1943 31

1944 36

1945 41

Glossary 46

Further resources 47

Index 48

Introduction

At the end of World War I in November 1918 Germany had been defeated. The Treaty of Versailles drawn up by the victors – Britain, France and the United States – was intended to prevent any future war in Europe. It cut Germany's army to 100,000 men and imposed huge fines on the Germans to compensate for the damage done during World War I. These payments were called reparations.

Germany had little money after the war. This meant it fell behind in its reparations payments. As punishment, France took over a part of Germany called the Ruhr, which was a key industrial centre. This caused a collapse of the German economy. Millions of Germans lost their jobs. The price of goods and food increased so quickly that many people could not afford enough food to eat. The German currency became worthless. In 1929 a worldwide economic collapse began, which left millions of Germans jobless. Many Germans were angry and confused. They blamed the Treaty of Versailles for many of their problems.

In such an atmosphere, many Germans were attracted to the extreme views of a former

In the 1930s, Hitler's Germany took over foreign lands that contained German-speaking peoples – the Sudetenland and Austria. Germany tried to take Polish land as well, which caused World War II.

THE EXPANSION OF GERMANY, 1933–1939

SWEDEN

ESTONIA

Baltic Sea

LATVIA

North Sea

DENMARK

LITHUANIA

EAST PRUSSIA

• Minsk

BRITAIN

NETHERLANDS

GERMANY

• Berlin

Warsaw •

POLAND

SOVIET UNION

London •

BELGIUM

LUXEMBOURG

• Prague

Sudetenland occupied 1938

CZECHOSLOVAKIA

• Paris

Vienna •

Czechoslovakia occupied 1939

FRANCE

Rhineland occupied 1936

SWITZERLAND

AUSTRIA

• Budapest

HUNGARY

Atlantic Ocean

Austria annexed 1938

ROMANIA

ITALY

Belgrade •

• Bucharest

YUGOSLAVIA

BULGARIA

• Rome

ALBANIA

Key

SPAIN

Mediterranean Sea

GREECE

German territory, 1933

0

400 miles

German territory by 1939

PORTUGAL

0

400 km

4

soldier named Adolf Hitler. Hitler's National Socialist German Workers' Party, or Nazi Party, blamed Germany's crisis on communists and Jews. So many people agreed with him that in 1933 Hitler became Germany's chancellor. Once in power, he created new jobs and built up the armed forces. This made him popular. But he also became a dictator, and persecuted Jews and communists.

The Treaty of Versailles had created new countries in Europe, such as Czechoslovakia. Many German-speaking people lived in these countries. Hitler was determined to make them citizens of Germany. He did this by taking over Czechoslovakia and Austria in the 1930s.

Italy and Japan

To the south, Italy had been ruled by the dictator Benito Mussolini since 1922. He also built up his country's armed forces and glorified war. It was natural, therefore, that Germany and Italy should become allies in the 1930s.

In East Asia, Japan had been on the winning side in World War I. However, Japan had had to give up Chinese lands it had conquered in an earlier war with Russia. The Japanese resented the fact that Britain and the United States treated them like a second-class nation. The Japanese also resented the fact that they had to buy nearly all their food, metal and oil from abroad. Like the European nations, they wanted colonies in the Far East that could provide these goods.

In the 1920s and 1930s Japan was determined to have an empire of its own to be a 'great power'. It also needed raw materials, such as oil and metal, to keep the navy running and build new weapons for the army. Japan attacked China in the 1930s. But Japan wanted more land and oil. This led to attacks on Britain and the United States in 1941.

Japan invaded Manchuria (a northern province of China) in 1931, and in 1937 invaded the rest of China. This was condemned by the League of Nations. The League was made up of many nations, but was led by Britain and France (the United States was not a member). The League criticised Germany, Italy and Japan for their aggression in the 1930s. But they ignored the League and formed their own alliance called the Rome-Berlin-Tokyo Axis. They were known as the Axis nations.

Hitler started threatening Poland about German lands that had passed to the Poles (land between Germany and East Prussia called the 'Polish Corridor'). Britain and France agreed to defend Poland against Germany. Hitler ignored them and attacked Poland on 1 September, 1939. World War II had begun.

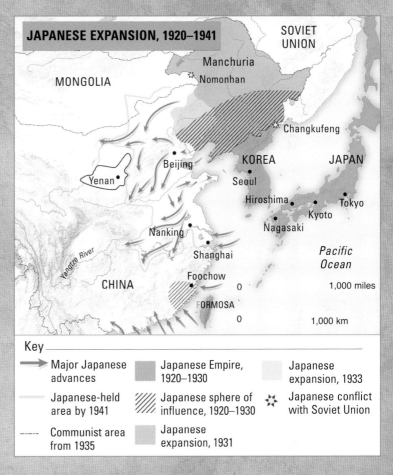

JAPANESE EXPANSION, 1920–1941

Key

→ Major Japanese advances

▬ Japanese-held area by 1941

---- Communist area from 1935

■ Japanese Empire, 1920–1930

/// Japanese sphere of influence, 1920–1930

■ Japanese expansion, 1931

□ Japanese expansion, 1933

✺ Japanese conflict with Soviet Union

18 JANUARY, 1919, France

The leaders of the victorious nations of World War I gather in Paris to talk about a treaty with the defeated countries of Germany and Austria-Hungary. These leaders include President Woodrow Wilson of the United States, British Prime Minister Lloyd George, French Prime Minister Georges Clemenceau and the Prime Minister of Italy, Vittorio Emanuele Orlando.

21 JANUARY, 1919, Ireland

Sinn Fein ('Ourselves Alone'), an Irish group that wants Ireland to be free from British rule, declares Ireland independent. This sparks a rebellion against the British. The British send 100,000 troops and paramilitaries (part-time soldiers) to Ireland to crush the revolt.

13 APRIL, 1919, India

In India, former lawyer Mahatma Gandhi is leading a campaign to free the country from British rule. A large crowd of Gandhi supporters gathers at Amritsar in the Punjab. British troops commanded by General Reginald Dyer open fire on the unarmed crowd, killing 379 people and wounding 1,208. The British authorities do not punish Dyer, which causes outrage throughout India.

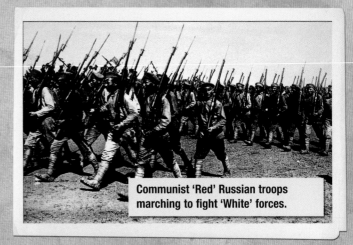

Communist 'Red' Russian troops marching to fight 'White' forces.

28 JUNE, 1919, France

The treaty produced at the talks in Paris is signed in the Hall of Mirrors at the Palace of Versailles. The Treaty of Versailles blames Germany for starting World War I and orders it to pay a huge fine.

21 JULY, 1919, Britain

German sailors deliberately sink, or scuttle, their ships at Scapa Flow in Britain's Orkney Islands. This is to stop the British making use of the German High Seas Fleet.

2 SEPTEMBER, 1919, Russia

In Russia, a civil war is raging between the 'Reds' (communists) and the 'Whites' (monarchists). The 'Whites' capture the

EYEWITNESS: Winston Churchill on the Amritsar Massacre, July 1920

"Unrest in India erupted into open violence. In April 1919, under the orders of General Dyer, troops opened fire on a crowd at Amritsar, killing 379 unarmed civilians and wounding over a thousand. The Commander-in-Chief in India recommended that General Dyer should be ordered to retire, and the matter came before the Army Council for review. The Council accepted the recommendation, as did the Cabinet."

Civil war – a war between opposing groups of citizens of the same country.

Ukrainian city of Kiev. Other 'White' troops under Peter Wrangel capture Tsaritsin (later Stalingrad) on 17 June, but are forced to retreat.

16–25 AUGUST, 1920, Poland

Polish troops attack 'Red' Russian armies near Warsaw. The Poles smash through the Russian centre, forcing the 'Reds' to retreat. Russian casualties total 150,000 men.

14 NOVEMBER, 1920, Russia

British warships evacuate Peter Wrangel's 'White' forces from the Crimea. The evacuation marks the end of the Russian Civil War and a 'Red' victory.

12 NOVEMBER, 1921, United States

The leading powers meet in Washington, D.C., to sign treaties aimed to prevent future wars. The Four-Power Act, signed on 13 December, agrees that Britain, France, Japan and the United States will peacefully solve any rival claims to land in the Pacific Ocean.

Italian fascist leader Benito Mussolini (second from right) in 1922.

28 OCTOBER, 1922, Italy

Fascist leader Benito Mussolini leads his followers, called 'Blackshirts', in the 'March on Rome'. He forces the government and king to give him complete power as a dictator. He begins a reign of terror against his opponents.

TURNING POINTS: The Treaty of Versailles

Versailles was a shock to the German delegation (seen right). Germany lost a tenth of its territory and population to France in the west and Poland in the east. The losses included the 'Polish Corridor'. This slice of territory gave Poland access to the Baltic Sea. Germany also had to accept the blame for starting World War I. The Germans had to pay a huge fine for the damage suffered by the victors. Finally, the mighty German Army was cut to 100,000 men.

Fascist – a supporter of a strongly nationalistic and militaristic political party.

TURNING POINTS: Extreme politics

Fascism and communism were extreme forms of right- and left-wing politics, respectively. Both were popular in the 1920s and 1930s in Europe. Germany (right) and Italy both had fascist leaders. They tried to make their countries strong by raising large armies and conquering other states. Russia was a communist country. It was prepared to use war to spread communism to other countries. Both fascism and communism turned people into slaves. Neither system allowed individuals any freedom.

9 NOVEMBER, 1923, Germany

Adolf Hitler leads the right-wing National Socialist German Workers' Party (Nazi Party) in an anti-government revolt in Munich. It fails. Hitler is sent to prison for five years, but serves only nine months.

26 MARCH, 1926, China

In China's civil war, Nationalist forces under General Chiang Kai-shek capture the city of Nanking. The Nationalists are trying to defeat the warlords and communists.

Armed members of Adolf Hitler's Nazi Party wearing swastika armbands.

28 JULY, 1930, China

Communist forces capture Chang-sha in central China, but the Nationalists retake the city. They begin 'bandit suppression' campaigns against the communists.

30 JANUARY, 1933, Germany

Nazi leader Adolf Hitler becomes chancellor (leader) of Germany following elections.

30 JUNE, 1934, Germany

More than 70 members of the Nazi Party are murdered on Adolf Hitler's orders. Hitler believes they are a threat to his absolute authority. The event is known as 'the Night of the Long Knives'.

3 OCTOBER, 1935, Ethiopia

Italian troops invade Ethiopia in eastern Africa. The surprise attack is part of Benito Mussolini's plan to create an Italian empire in Africa.

Warlord – a military commander who has political power over a region.

EYEWITNESS: Noel Monks, British journalist, on the bombing of Guernica

"I was the first correspondent to reach Guernica, and was immediately pressed into service by some Basque soldiers collecting charred bodies that the flames had passed over. Some of the soldiers were sobbing like children. There were flames and smoke and grit. Houses were collapsing into the inferno. The only things left standing were a church, a sacred tree and, just outside the town, a small munitions factory."

15 AUGUST, 1936, Spain
The Spanish Civil War begins when troops in Spain and in Spanish Morocco rebel against Manuel Azãna's Republican government. General Francisco Franco leads the rebels, who become known as Nationalists.

25 APRIL, 1937, Spain
German aircraft, part of the Condor Legion that is fighting on the side of the Nationalists, bomb the town of Guernica. Some 1,600 civilians are killed and nearly 900 wounded.

7 JULY, 1937, China
Japanese troops attack Chinese units at the Marco Polo Bridge near Beijing. The attack is part of Japan's plan to take over China and get access to its resources.

12 MARCH, 1938, Germany
Hitler orders the German takeover of Austria, where some six million Germans live. Many Austrians welcome the move, which is completed the next day. Italian leader Benito Mussolini also supports German *Anschluss* ('Union') with Austria.

11 JULY, 1938, China
Fighting breaks out between the Soviet Union and Japan, which is occupying Manchuria and Korea. The Soviets beat off the Japanese attacks by mid-August.

29 SEPTEMBER, 1938, Germany
Adolf Hitler meets Italian leader Benito Mussolini, British Prime Minister Neville Chamberlain and Édouard Daladier, France's Prime Minister, at Munich. Hitler wants to take over Czechoslovakia, where many Germans live. Britain and France agree to his demands, believing that this will bring peace. The Sudetenland region of Czechoslovakia becomes part of Germany.

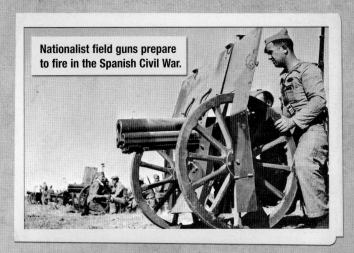

Nationalist field guns prepare to fire in the Spanish Civil War.

Rebel – someone who fights against a government or leader.

9–10 NOVEMBER, 1938, Germany

Nazis attack German Jews and their property, particularly synagogues. The attacks become known as *Kristallnacht* ('Crystal Night') because of the glass from smashed windows that litters the roads and pavements. People outside Germany – and many Germans – are horrified.

26 JANUARY, 1939, Spain

Nationalists capture Barcelona, the Republican-held capital of Catalonia.

10 MARCH, 1939, Czechoslovakia

Adolf Hitler begins the takeover of Bohemia and Moravia, parts of Czechoslovakia where many Germans live. The operation is completed by 16 March. Czechoslovakia ceases to exist.

28 MARCH, 1939, Spain

Nationalist troops enter the capital, Madrid. They have won the civil war. The civil war

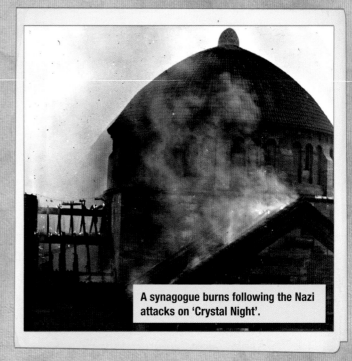

A synagogue burns following the Nazi attacks on 'Crystal Night'.

has cost the lives of some 300,000 Spaniards. Nationalist leader General Francisco Franco is now ruler of Spain.

22 MAY, 1939, Italy

The government agrees closer military ties with Germany. The stronger alliance

TURNING POINTS: Appeasement

Appeasement began in the early 1930s in Britain and France. Politicians such as British leader Neville Chamberlain (left of picture) and French minister Édouard Daladier thought that Adolf Hitler's demands for the return of 'German' areas were fair. They argued that if they gave in to Hitler he would not go to war. But Hitler saw their attitude as proof that Britain and France were weak. It convinced him that if he went to war they would not interfere.

Appeasement – avoiding conflict by giving in to someone's demands.

EYEWITNESS: K.S. Karol, Polish cadet, September 1939

"The smell along the road was unchanging. It was the smell of dead horses that no one had bothered to bury and that stank to high heaven. We moved only at night and we learned to sleep while marching; smoking was forbidden out of fear that the glow off a cigarette could bring down on us the all-powerful Luftwaffe. But along the roads, day or night, we were never alone; other soldiers and civilians were also marching."

between the two countries becomes known as the 'Pact of Steel'.

23 AUGUST Germany
Germany signs a non-aggression pact with the Soviet Union. The Soviets agree not to oppose a German invasion of Poland. In return, they and the Germans will divide Poland between them.

1 SEPTEMBER Poland
A German force of 53 divisions, supported by 1,600 aircraft, invades Poland. Poland has few tanks and aircraft. The Poles are quickly overwhelmed.

2 SEPTEMBER Britain and France
Britain and France both threaten war if Germany does not withdraw immediately from Poland. The Germans ignore the demands.

3 SEPTEMBER Britain and France
Britain, France, Australia and New Zealand declare war on Nazi Germany.

3 SEPTEMBER Atlantic Ocean
The German submarine *U-30* mistakes the British liner *Athenia* for a warship. The submarine sinks the ship. Some 112 civilian passengers drown.

6 SEPTEMBER Poland
The Polish government and high command flee Warsaw. They order Polish forces to withdraw to the south of the country. Nazi troops advance to Lódz, near Warsaw, and capture Cracow.

German troops tear down a border post as they advance into Poland.

Division – an army unit made up of 15,000 to 20,000 soldiers.

8 SEPTEMBER Poland

The German Tenth Army reaches the outskirts of Warsaw, the capital. Elsewhere, the German Fourteenth Army reaches Przemysl. General Heinz Guderian's panzer (tank) units advance east of Warsaw as far as the River Bug.

9 SEPTEMBER Poland

The Poles launch a counter-attack against the German Eighth Army to the south of Warsaw. The attack over the River Bzura is initially a success. But then the Germans counter-attack and are able to push back the Polish troops.

10 SEPTEMBER France

Troops of the British Expeditionary Force (BEF) begin to land in France to help the French fight the Germans. Some 160,000 men and 24,000 vehicles arrive during the course of September.

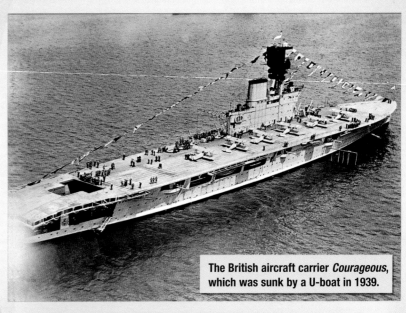

The British aircraft carrier *Courageous*, which was sunk by a U-boat in 1939.

17 SEPTEMBER Atlantic Ocean

The British aircraft carrier HMS *Courageous* is sunk by the German submarine *U-29*. The aircraft carrier *Ark Royal* has escaped a similar submarine attack just three days earlier. The naval high command orders Britain's aircraft carriers into port to save them from being sunk.

KEY PEOPLE: Adolf Hitler

Adolf Hitler (1889–1945) was the German leader of the Nazi Party. He thought that Germany's economic problems could be overcome by the conquest of other lands and by expelling Jews and other groups from Germany. Hitler was elected chancellor in 1933 and made himself *Führer*, or supreme leader, of the Third Reich. Hitler began World War II when he invaded Poland in 1939. Facing defeat in 1945, he took his own life.

Expeditionary force – an army sent to serve abroad.

17–30 SEPTEMBER Poland

Under the terms of a secret clause in the 1939 pact with Germany, the Soviet Red Army invades Poland. It meets little resistance on Poland's eastern border. The Polish Army is fighting for its life in the west.

18–30 SEPTEMBER Poland

Poland is defeated. The Polish government and high command flee to Romania, where they are imprisoned. A government-in-exile is formed and many Poles escape to Britain and France. Poland is split into two zones of occupation, one German, one Russian. Germany has lost 10,572 troops and the Soviet Union has lost 734 men killed in the campaign. Around 50,000 Poles are killed and 750,000 captured.

27 SEPTEMBER Germany

Adolf Hitler tells his senior generals of his plans for an attack against France, Belgium and Holland. The attack will take place this year. The generals object to Hitler making plans without their knowledge. They argue that Germany is not ready to launch such an attack. In the event, the attack is constantly delayed due to bad weather.

29 SEPTEMBER USSR

After occupying Poland, the Soviet Union aims to extend its control over the Baltic coast. It hopes to reduce the chance of any German threat. During the next few weeks the Soviets gain bases and sign 'mutual assistance' agreements with Lithuania, Latvia and Estonia. Finland, however, will not agree to Soviet demands. It prepares its army to meet a Soviet attack.

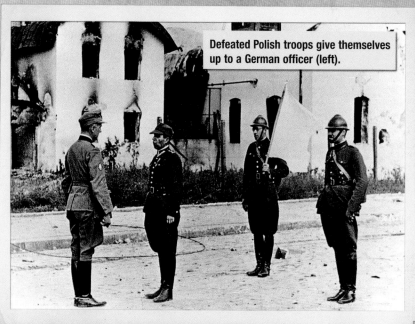

Defeated Polish troops give themselves up to a German officer (left).

Occupation – military control of part of a country by forces from another.

13

EYEWITNESS: Leland Stowe, Oslo, 9 April, 1940

"Less than fifteen hundred German soldiers had occupied Norway's capital while thousands of dazed, bewildered citizens looked dumbly on. Not a bomb had been dropped inside Oslo. This handful of troops had arrived by air, since daybreak that morning. They had only small weapons — but absolutely incredible discipline and nerve. They were an amazingly tiny band of men, but they marched in like conquerors. They were."

14 OCTOBER North Sea

The battleship HMS *Royal Oak* is sunk in the British base at Scapa Flow in the Orkney Islands. The U-boat attack costs 786 lives. Defences at the base are improved.

30 NOVEMBER Finland

A Soviet force of more than 600,000 men attacks Finland. Soviet aircraft bomb the capital, Helsinki. Field Marshal Karl von Mannerheim leads Finland's defence with a force consisting mainly of reservists. The Finns are inferior in numbers and weapons to the Soviets, but the main Soviet attack is held at the Mannerheim Line. This system of defences was built during World War I (1914–18) through rugged terrain and forest. As the war progresses, Finnish ski troops launch hit-and-run raids on Red Army troops, who are struggling because they have no winter clothing.

2 DECEMBER Finland

The League of Nations tries to stop the war in Finland. The Soviet Union is a member of the League, but rejects its involvement. The League expels the Soviets on 14 December.

16 DECEMBER Finland

After advancing to the Mannerheim Line, the Soviets attack again. The Finns have few tanks and little artillery. They use home-made 'Molotov Cocktails' (bottles filled with gasoline) to destroy enemy tanks.

The German pocket battleship *Graf Spee* burns before it is scuttled.

13 DECEMBER Atlantic Ocean

In the Battle of the River Plate, British warships fight the German pocket battleship *Graf Spee* at the mouth of the River Plate, off Uruguay. The British vessels are damaged, but the *Graf Spee* is forced to withdraw to neutral Uruguay for repairs. British ships trap it in port. The *Graf Spee* is scuttled (sunk) by its crew on 17 December.

Reservists – part of an army called on to fight in an emergency.

16 FEBRUARY, 1940, Norway

The British destroyer HMS *Cossack* enters neutral waters off Norway to rescue 299 British merchant sailors held on the German transport *Altmark*.

11 MARCH Soviet Union

Finland and the Soviet Union agree a treaty to end the war between them. Finland loses 10 percent of its territory to the Soviets. War losses are 200,000 Soviet troops and 25,000 Finns.

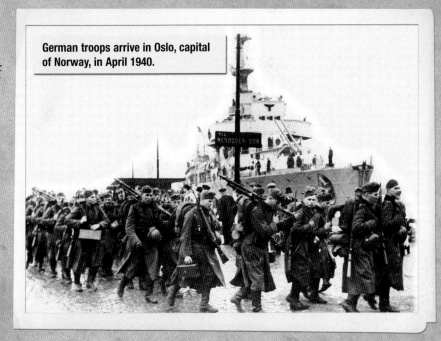

German troops arrive in Oslo, capital of Norway, in April 1940.

9 APRIL Norway and Denmark

A German invasion force, including warships and 1,000 aircraft, attacks Denmark and Norway. Denmark is overrun immediately. Although Norwegian forces resist, they have no tanks and little artillery. Their coastal defences and navy are also very poor.

14–19 APRIL Norway

More than 10,000 Allied troops land to help the Norwegians fight the Germans.

7–10 MAY Britain

Prime Minister Neville Chamberlain resigns. Winston Churchill replaces him.

TURNING POINTS: *Blitzkrieg*

Blitzkrieg is a German term meaning 'lightning war'. It was a military tactic that aimed to defeat an enemy by a single, fast attack. *Blitzkrieg* required many tanks (right), mobile artillery and aircraft. *Blitzkrieg* always avoided enemy strongpoints. Instead, it targeted enemy rear areas where supplies were located. German infantry surrounded enemy troops and forced them to surrender. German planes destroyed most enemy aircraft on the ground in the war's first few days.

Pocket battleship – a powerful warship smaller than a battleship.

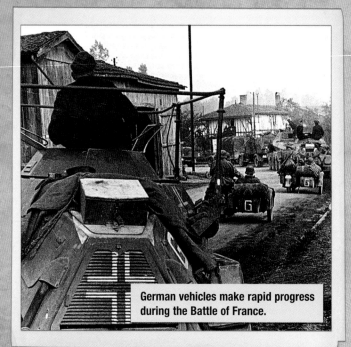

German vehicles make rapid progress during the Battle of France.

12–14 MAY France

German tanks smash through the forested Ardennes region in eastern France and advance west. They open a 75-kilometre (50-mile) gap in the Allied frontline. This drives a wedge between the Allied armies in France and those in Belgium.

26 MAY France

Operation Dynamo begins to evacuate Allied forces who have retreated to the port of Dunkirk. An assorted fleet of pleasure boats, commercial craft and naval vessels crosses and recrosses the English Channel to rescue the troops from the beaches.

10 MAY Holland and Belgium

Nazi paratroopers seize Belgium's key frontier fortress, Eben Emael, and land in Holland. British and French armies advance into Belgium to meet what they think is the main German assault. However, the main German attack will take place to the south, in the Ardennes.

28 MAY Belgium

King Leopold of Belgium surrenders. His forces are surrounded after the Allied withdrawal to Dunkirk.

31 MAY United States

President Franklin D. Roosevelt launches a huge arms-building 'defence programme'.

KEY PEOPLE: Winston Churchill

Winston Spencer Churchill (1874–1965) was one of World War II's major personalities. He was a former soldier, journalist and politician who became British prime minister in 1940. The Nazis seemed close to victory, but he helped turn British fortunes around. He dismissed any sign of defeatism and rallied the nation to keep fighting. Churchill also made strong alliances with the United States and appointed fine generals to run the war.

Evacuation – the removal of people from a dangerous area.

EYEWITNESS: General Erwin Rommel, France, May 1940

"The tanks now rolled in a long column through the line of fortifications and on towards the first houses, which had been set alight by our fire. In the moonlight we could see the men of 7th Motorcycle Battalion moving forward on foot beside us. Occasionally an enemy machine-gun or anti-tank gun fired, but none of their shots came anywhere near us. Our artillery was dropping heavy fire on villages and the road."

4–9 JUNE Norway
British and French troops begin to leave Norway. King Haakon and the government leave for Britain on the 7th. The king orders Norwegian forces to stop fighting on 9 June, after losing 1,335 men in the war. Total Allied losses are 5,600. German losses total 3,692 men.

3–4 JUNE France
Operation Dynamo ends. The 'little ships' have rescued 338,226 men – two-thirds of them British – from the beaches of Dunkirk.

5–12 JUNE France
The Germans launch Operation Red, a drive toward the capital, Paris. Some French troops fight bravely, but many units lack men, supplies and guns. The French begin to withdraw south. Their morale crumbles.

10 JUNE Italy
Italy declares war on France and Britain. Benito Mussolini, Italy's fascist leader, is eager to take advantage of France's collapse. Canada declares war on Italy on the 10th; Australia, New Zealand and South Africa follow the next day.

14 JUNE France
The French declare Paris an 'open city' – meaning that they will not defend it – in order to save it from destruction. German troops enter the city unopposed.

16–24 JUNE France
New prime minister Marshal Henri-Philippe Pétain takes power and promises to request a peace treaty with Germany. The treaty leaves Germany in control of two-thirds of France, including the Channel and Atlantic coasts. The south, now known as Vichy France, will be under French rule. French casualties since 10 May are 85,000, British 3,475 and German 27,074.

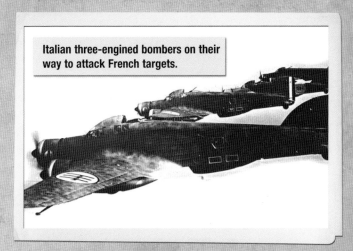
Italian three-engined bombers on their way to attack French targets.

Morale – the emotional well-being of people.

TURNING POINTS: The Battle of Britain

The Battle of Britain was Germany's attempt to win control of the skies over England and the Channel. Victory in the air was necessary before any invasion began. The Germans had 2,800 aircraft that set out to destroy Britain's 700 fighters. Britain's fate rested on 'the Few' – the pilots who flew Hurricane (right) and Spitfire fighters. On 31 October, after 114 days of combat, Germany gave in. The Germans had lost 1,733 aircraft. The RAF had lost 828 aircraft – but had saved Britain's air defences.

30 JUNE Channel Islands

German troops invade the Channel Islands. The islands are the only British home territory occupied during the war.

1 JULY Atlantic Ocean

Using French ports as bases, U-boats inflict serious losses on Allied convoys carrying supplies across the Atlantic. This so-called 'Happy Time' lasts until October.

3 JULY Algeria

Fearing that they will be used by Germany, British warships attack French vessels at Oran and Mers-el-Kebir, Algeria. French naval forces in Alexandria, Egypt, are disarmed on the 7th. Meanwhile, two French battleships, nine destroyers and other craft are captured in Britain.

10 JULY Britain

The Battle of Britain begins. Hermann Goering, the Nazi Air Force chief, orders attacks on Allied shipping and ports in the English Channel. The air attacks soon reduce the movement of Allied ships in the English Channel.

Allied vessels under German air attack in the English Channel.

Convoy – a number of ships or vehicles travelling together.

16 JULY Germany

Hitler reveals a plan to invade Britain, codenamed Operation Sealion. It requires control of Channel ports where the invasion force can board ships. British warplanes must also be destroyed so that the troops can cross the Channel safely.

21 JULY Soviet Union

The Soviets annexe (take over) Lithuania, Latvia and Estonia.

13–17 AUGUST Britain

'Eagle Day' begins a four-day German air attack against British airfields and factories.

24–25 AUGUST Britain

The Luftwaffe inflicts serious losses on the RAF in attacks on its bases in southeast England. Fighter Command, which runs the British air war, is close to breaking point.

A German Heinkel bomber flies over London during the 'Blitz'.

26–29 AUGUST Germany

The RAF launches night raids on Berlin and other cities. The Germans bomb London in revenge, but the raids mean that many German aircraft remain in Germany.

7 SEPTEMBER Britain

Full-scale bombing raids on London – the 'Blitz' – begin; the city is initially bombed for 57 consecutive days.

13–18 SEPTEMBER Egypt

An Italian force of 250,000 invades British-controlled Egypt and advances slowly.

20–22 SEPTEMBER Atlantic Ocean

German U-boats launch their first 'Wolf Pack' operation, sinking 12 Allied ships. A 'pack' brings together some 15 to 20 U-boats for an attack on a convoy.

EYEWITNESS: John Beard, RAF pilot, Battle of Britain

"I saw my first burst (of gunfire) go in and, just as I was on top of him and turning away, I noticed a red glow inside the bomber. I turned tightly into position again and now saw several short tongues of flame lick out along the fuselage. Then he went down in a spin, blanketed with smoke and with pieces flying off."

'Wolf Pack' – a group of 15 to 20 German U-boats.

27 SEPTEMBER Germany, Italy and Japan

All three countries agree the Tripartite Pact. They will all fight any state that declares war on any one of them.

28 OCTOBER Greece

Italy demands to be allowed to occupy Greece for as long as the war lasts. Italian troops invade Greece from Albania, meeting Greek resistance.

5 NOVEMBER United States

President Franklin D. Roosevelt is elected for an unprecedented third term.

11–12 NOVEMBER Mediterranean Sea

The Battle of Taranto. British torpedo aircraft destroy three Italian battleships and damage two vessels. British cruisers also sink four vessels in the Strait of Otranto.

14 NOVEMBER Britain

The industrial city of Coventry is bombed by 449 German aircraft. The raid kills 500 civilians and leaves thousands homeless.

A German photograph of Coventry. This English city was bombed in 1940.

9–11 DECEMBER Egypt

The British begin their first offensive in North Africa. The Western Desert Force – 31,000 men supported by aircraft and naval gunfire – attacks Italian positions. Some 34,000 Italians are taken prisoner as they retreat rapidly from Egypt.

KEY PEOPLE: Benito Mussolini

Benito Mussolini (1883–1945) was the fascist dictator of Italy. After coming to power in 1922, he put down opposition and promised to create a new Roman empire. He followed his ally, Adolf Hitler, into World War II. Soon, however, Italy suffered a number of defeats. It had to depend on German military help. In July 1943, Mussolini was sacked by the king. He was rescued by German troops, but shot by Italian communists in April 1945.

Ultimatum – a demand made by one country on another.

EYEWITNESS: Ernie Pyle, U.S. journalist, London, 1940

"Shortly after the sirens wailed you could hear the Germans grinding overhead. In my room, with its black curtains drawn across the windows, you could feel the shake from the guns. You could hear the boom, crump, crump, crump, of heavy bombs at their work of tearing buildings apart. They were not too far away. Flames seemed to whip hundreds of feet into the air. St. Paul's was surrounded by fire, but it came through."

2 JANUARY, 1941, United States
President Franklin D. Roosevelt announces a programme to produce 200 freighters, called 'Liberty' ships, to support the Allied Atlantic convoys.

3 FEBRUARY Atlantic Ocean
The German battlecruisers *Scharnhorst* and *Gneisenau* start sinking Allied merchant ships in the Atlantic. They sink 22 vessels before returning to base on 22 March.

14 FEBRUARY North Africa
German General Erwin Rommel's skilled Afrika Korps arrives at Tripoli in Libya to help the Italians.

11 MARCH United States
President Franklin D. Roosevelt signs the Lend-Lease Act. The act allows Britain to obtain supplies without having to pay for them immediately in cash.

28–29 MARCH Mediterranean Sea
The Battle of Cape Matapan. The Italian and British fleets clash in the Aegean Sea. Five Italian ships are sunk and 3,000 men killed. The British lose just one aircraft.

6–15 APRIL Yugoslavia
German forces, with Italian and Hungarian support, invade Yugoslavia.

17 APRIL Yugoslavia
Yugoslavia surrenders to Germany. But guerrilla forces, called partisans, continue to resist the occupiers.

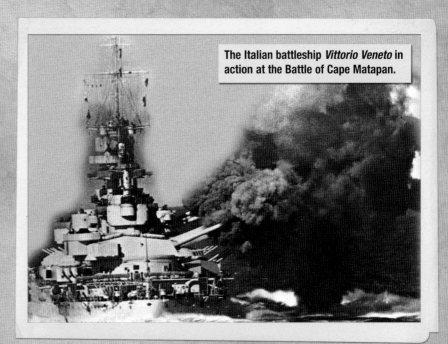

The Italian battleship *Vittorio Veneto* in action at the Battle of Cape Matapan.

Partisan – a soldier who fights behind enemy lines.

TURNING POINTS: Lend-Lease

After the fall of France in June 1940, U.S. President Franklin D. Roosevelt wanted to supply Britain with weapons to keep fighting Germany. Britain could not afford to pay, however. In March 1941, the U.S. Congress passed the Lend-Lease Act. The act gave Roosevelt power to supply goods (including ships, right) and services to countries friendly to the United States. The other countries did not have to pay right away. Almost $13 billion of goods had been allocated under the arrangement by November 1941.

18–21 APRIL Greece

Greek positions are collapsing rapidly as the Germans advance. British troops sent to help the Greeks are also falling back to the southern coast to be evacuated to Crete.

3–19 MAY Ethiopia

The Battle of Amba Alagi in northern Ethiopia ends in Italian surrender to the British. Some 230,000 Italians have been killed or captured in East Africa.

10 MAY Britain

Rudolf Hess, deputy leader of Germany, flies secretly to Scotland on an unofficial mission to ask Britain to allow Germany a 'free hand' in Europe. In return, the Nazis will leave Britain and its empire alone. The British imprison him.

10–11 MAY Britain

In the largest raid of the 'Blitz', London is attacked by 507 bombers. Since September 1940, 39,678 people have died and 46,119 people have been injured by the raids.

20–22 MAY Crete

Some 23,000 German paratroopers attack Crete. They come under attack from the 42,000 British, New Zealand, Australian and Greek troops on the island. But the Germans gain enough of a footing to allow them to land reinforcements.

The German battleship *Bismarck* opens fire on the British ship HMS *Hood*.

Paratrooper – a soldier who jumps from an aircraft with a parachute.

EYEWITNESS: Esmond Knight, HMS *Prince of Wales*, 24 May, 1941

"I just did not believe what I saw – *Hood* had literally been blown to pieces, and just before she was totally enveloped in that ghastly pall of smoke I noticed that she was firing her last salvo. I felt quite sick inside and turned away and looked towards George, where he was standing with his hands limply to his sides, staring like a man in a dream."

23–27 MAY Atlantic Ocean
British warships find the German battleship *Bismarck* in the Denmark Straits between Iceland and Greenland. The *Bismarck* sinks the battlecruiser *Hood* and damages the battleship *Prince of Wales* – but is then sunk by gunfire and torpedoes.

28–31 MAY Crete
The Germans capture Crete. British losses are 3,753 men, while Germany has 3,985 men killed or missing.

15–17 JUNE North Africa
The British launch Operation Battleaxe to relieve the Libyan port of Tobruk, where British troops are surrounded by the Afrika Korps. The operation halts after the British lose 90 of their 190 tanks.

22 JUNE Soviet Union
Germany launches Operation Barbarossa, the invasion of the Soviet Union, with three million men. Army Group North strikes toward the Baltic and Leningrad. Army Group Centre aims to take Smolensk and then Moscow. Army Group South advances toward the Ukraine and the Caucasus.

German air attacks quickly destroy 1,800 Soviet aircraft on the ground.

4 JULY Yugoslavia
Joseph Broz, known as 'Tito', emerges as the leader of the Yugoslav partisans.

16 JULY Soviet Union
Around 300,000 Red Army troops and 3,200 tanks are trapped near Smolensk.

31 JULY Germany
Reinhard Heydrich, head of the SS secret police, is ordered to plan the destruction of Europe's Jews. This 'Final Solution' will lead to the killing of millions of people.

Soviet soldiers surrender to German troops during Operation Barbarossa.

Surrender – to stop fighting and give in to the enemy.

Female recruits to the Soviet forces march through Moscow.

British tanks suffer heavy losses to German anti-tank guns, but Rommel retreats. This relieves the pressure on Tobruk.

26 NOVEMBER Pacific Ocean
A Japanese fleet of six aircraft carriers and other warships begins a mission to destroy the U.S. Pacific Fleet at Pearl Harbor, Hawaii. The ships remain undetected by maintaining radio silence. Japan's war aims are to destroy U.S. warships in the region and then to seize lands in the Pacific and East Asia. The Japanese intend to create a 'Greater East Asian Co-Prosperity Sphere' to supply Japan with resources.

3 SEPTEMBER Poland
Successful experiments to kill Jewish prisoners using gas chambers are carried out in Auschwitz concentration camp. They will lead to the widespread use of Zyclon-B gas to kill Jews.

4 SEPTEMBER Atlantic Ocean
A U-boat mistakes the U.S. destroyer *Greer* for a British vessel and attacks it. U.S. warships are ordered to 'shoot on sight' any U-boats they see.

19 SEPTEMBER Soviet Union
The Germans capture Kiev, killing or capturing 665,000 Soviet soldiers.

30 SEPTEMBER Soviet Union
The Germans begin Operation Typhoon, the attack on Moscow.

18–26 NOVEMBER North Africa
The British Eighth Army in Egypt launches Operation Crusader to relieve Tobruk.

EYEWITNESS: Major Lozak, Leningrad, December 1941

"I have lived in Leningrad all my life. I'd walk for a while, and then sit down for a rest. Many a time I saw a man suddenly collapse on the snow. There was nothing I could do. One just walked on. And, on the way back, I would see a vague human form covered with snow on the spot where, in the morning, I had seen a man fall down."

U-boat – a German submarine.

TURNING POINTS: Rationing

The war brought international trade to a near halt. Countries such as Britain could not import enough food. In the Soviet Union, where farmland was damaged by fighting, thousands of people starved to death. All the countries involved in the war introduced rationing, which limited how much food people could buy. People had ration books that allowed them to get a set amount of food each day or week. As the war went on, food and water (right) became more difficult to get. Rations were cut.

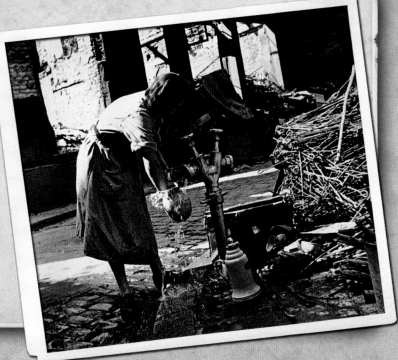

7 DECEMBER Hawaii

Some 183 Japanese aircraft attack the U.S. Pacific Fleet at Pearl Harbor, Hawaii. They destroy six battleships and 188 aircraft, damage or sink 10 other vessels and kill 2,000 people. The Japanese lose 29 aircraft.

U.S. warships on fire at Pearl Harbor following the Japanese attack.

8 DECEMBER Soviet Union

Adolf Hitler halts the advance on Moscow for the winter. The German panzers cannot operate in the freezing temperatures.

10 DECEMBER Pacific Ocean

About 90 Japanese aircraft sink the British warships *Prince of Wales* and *Repulse*: 730 sailors drown.

11 DECEMBER Germany and Italy

Germany and Italy declare war on the United States. The United States then declares war on Germany and Italy.

18–19 DECEMBER Egypt

An Italian attack on the British Mediterranean Fleet in Alexandria, Egypt, sinks the battleships *Queen Elizabeth* and *Valiant*. The Italians use 'human torpedoes', midget submarines each driven by two operators.

Panzer – German word for a tank.

5 JANUARY, 1942, Soviet Union

Joseph Stalin orders a massive counterattack against the German invaders. The Red Army has initial success and captures trains, food and munitions. But then German forces set up well-defended areas known as 'hedgehogs', which halt the Soviet attacks.

10–11 JANUARY Dutch East Indies

Japanese troops attack the Dutch East Indies to capture the oilfields of the island chain.

13 JANUARY Atlantic Ocean

Germany's U-boats launch Operation Drum Roll, a series of attacks on shipping off the east coast of the United States. Some 20 ships are sunk in the first month.

16–19 JANUARY Germany

Hitler sacks more than 30 of his senior generals; he is impatient that they want to withdraw in the face of Soviet attacks on the Eastern Front.

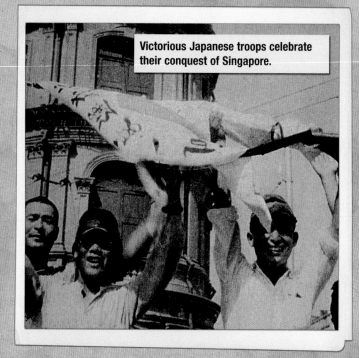

Victorious Japanese troops celebrate their conquest of Singapore.

20 JANUARY Germany

The Wannsee Conference in Berlin. SS deputy leader Reinhard Heydrich reveals his plans for what is termed the 'Final Solution' to the so-called 'Jewish problem'. The extermination of Jews in Europe becomes central to Nazi war plans.

KEY WEAPONS: Atlantic convoys

Convoys helped protect Allied merchant ships against enemy attack. A large group – often more than 50 vessels – was accompanied by warships. The main threat to convoys came from U-boats, but antisubmarine measures gradually improved. Cooperation between naval and air forces also improved. It was helped by new tactics and innovations, such as radar. In the North Atlantic alone, the Germans sank 2,232 Allied vessels. But they lost 785 U-boats in return.

Extermination – the murder of an entire people.

The German heavy cruiser *Prinz Eugen* during the 'Channel Dash'.

8 FEBRUARY Singapore

Japanese troops land on the British-held island of Singapore. The British surrender on 14 February when the water supply is cut. The defenders have lost 138,000 men.

11–12 FEBRUARY North Sea

In the so-called Channel Dash, the German battlecruisers *Gneisenau* and *Scharnhorst* and the heavy cruiser *Prinz Eugen* leave Brest. They speed through the English Channel into the North Sea before British warships and aircraft can stop them.

27–29 FEBRUARY Java Sea

The Battle of the Java Sea. Five Allied cruisers and nine destroyers fight 17 Japanese warships. Five Allied cruisers and five destroyers are sunk. The Japanese lose only one cruiser in this victory.

28–29 MARCH France

British commandos attack the St. Nazaire dry-dock, used by the Germans to repair warships. The British fill an old destroyer and ram the lock gates, blowing them up. But 144 men die in the raid and many more are captured.

9 APRIL Philippines

Major General Jonathan Wainwright, commanding the U.S. and Filipino forces, surrenders to the Japanese. Some 78,000 U.S. and Filipino troops are forced to make a 104-kilometre (65-mile) march without food or water. Many die along the way.

18 APRIL Japan

Lieutenant Colonel James Doolittle leads 16 U.S. B-25 bombers, launched from the aircraft carrier *Hornet*, on a daring mission to strike targets in Japan, including the capital Tokyo. The raid alarms Japan's leaders, who decide to seek a battle to destroy U.S. naval power in the Pacific.

EYEWITNESS: Robert Carse, British merchant seaman, 1942

"They came early: the Heinkels, the Messerschmitts, the Stukas, the Junkers 89s, and all told there were 105 of them over us during that day's fight that was to last twenty hours. All around us, as so slowly we kept on going, the pure blue of the sea was mottled blackish with the greasy patches of their bomb discharges. Our ship was missed closely time and again. We drew our breaths in a kind of gasping-choke."

Commandos – special forces soldiers.

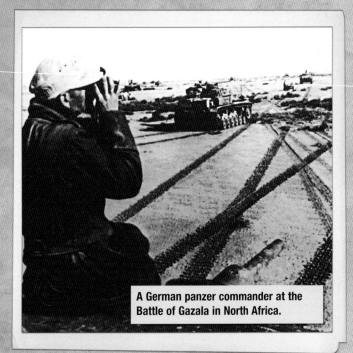

A German panzer commander at the Battle of Gazala in North Africa.

Rommel has 630 tanks, but they suffer serious fuel problems until the Italians break through the British Gazala Line to bring up fuel supplies on the 31st.

31 MAY Germany

Britain launches its first '1,000 bomber raid' on Cologne, where 59,000 people are left homeless. The British lose 40 aircraft.

4 JUNE Pacific Ocean

The Battle of Midway. Japan's fleet of 165 warships, including eight carriers, aims to seize the U.S. base at Midway Island and destroy the U.S. Pacific Fleet. The U.S. Navy has fewer ships, but has managed to gather three carriers. In the battle, the Japanese lose four carriers and 275 aircraft.

8 MAY Pacific Ocean

In the Battle of the Coral Sea, the U.S. Navy loses a carrier. The Japanese lose a smaller carrier, but large numbers of aircraft.

10–13 JUNE North Africa

The Battle of Gazala. German attacks force the British Eighth Army to withdraw east. Rommel's way is open to Tobruk.

26–31 MAY North Africa

The Battle of Gazala. Rommel attacks the British Eighth Army, which has 850 tanks.

KEY PEOPLE: Joseph Stalin

Joseph Stalin (1879–1953) was the communist dictator of the Soviet Union. He was stunned when his ally Hitler invaded in June 1941, but called on Russians to defend 'Mother Russia'. Stalin demanded that Britain and the United States open a 'second front' in western Europe to relieve the Soviet Union. The Allies also sent him supplies. After the war, Stalin created communist 'buffer states' around the Soviet Union.

'Buffer state' – a country between two enemy states.

EYEWITNESS: Mitsuo Fuchida on the *Akagi*, Battle of Midway, 1942

"The raiders closed in from both sides, barely skimming over the water. Flying in single columns, they were within five miles and seemed to be aiming straight for *Akagi*. I watched in breathless suspense, thinking how impossible it would be to dodge all their torpedoes. But these raiders, too, without protective escorts, were already being engaged by our fighters. There was wild cheering and whistling as the raiders went."

21 JUNE North Africa
Rommel captures Tobruk. Some 30,000 men are seized, together with rations and fuel.

28 JUNE Soviet Union
Germany launches Operation Blue, a summer offensive into southern Russia. Its target is the Russian oilfields in the Caucasus region.

4–10 JULY Soviet Union
After a two-month siege, the Germans capture the port of Sevastopol. About 90,000 Red Army troops are taken prisoner.

7–21 AUGUST Guadalcanal
The U.S. 1st Marine Division lands on Guadalcanal. Fierce fighting breaks out against Japanese defenders to control the airstrip at Henderson Field.

9 AUGUST Pacific Ocean
The Battle of Savo Island. The Japanese sink four U.S. cruisers. This is a heavy defeat for the U.S. Navy in the Pacific.

19 AUGUST France
A force of 5,000 Canadian, 1,000 British and 50 U.S. troops attack the port of Dieppe. It is a disaster: 4,000 men are killed or captured.

23 AUGUST Soviet Union
A raid by 600 German bombers on Stalingrad claims thousands of lives.

2 SEPTEMBER Poland
The Nazis are 'clearing' the Jewish Warsaw Ghetto. Over 50,000 Jews have been killed.

The Japanese carrier *Hiryu* under U.S. air attack at the Battle of Midway.

Ghetto – part of a city where Jews were forced to live.

TURNING POINTS: Strategic Bombing

Strategic bombing is the name given to air attacks against an enemy's industry and population. However, while the Allied strategic bombing of Germany's oil industry and transportation system played a key role near the end of the war, the bombers (right) were never capable of defeating the enemy alone. Raids against Japan began in 1944. They reduced a number of cities to ashes – but Japan did not surrender until the nuclear strikes in 1945.

23 OCTOBER North Africa

The Battle of El Alamein begins when 195,000 Allied troops attack 104,000 Axis soldiers. Axis resistance is fierce.

2–24 NOVEMBER North Africa

The Battle of El Alamein. Rommel is forced to retreat. Germany and Italy have lost 59,000 men killed, wounded or captured. The Allies have suffered 13,000 losses. El Alamein is the first major defeat suffered by German forces during the war.

19 NOVEMBER Soviet Union

General Georgi Zhukov launches a Soviet attack to relieve the city of Stalingrad, which is occupied by the Germans. The rapid pincer movement traps the Germans fighting in the city. The German front collapses.

19 DECEMBER Soviet Union

German attempts fail to rescue the Sixth Army trapped in Stalingrad. Within the city, German troops are suffering severe hardships due to the bitterly cold winter weather and food shortages.

Soldiers of the British Eighth Army attacking at the Battle of El Alamein.

Strategic – something that is useful in achieving a long-term goal.

EYEWITNESS: General Theodore Roosevelt, North Africa, March 1943

"Among our troubles were the dive-bombers. They came down on us constantly. Once I was caught in a valley by a raid. A bomb hit within twelve paces of where I was lying. My helmet was struck by a fragment and knocked galley-west, but I was unhurt though a couple of men were killed. The following day the enemy counter-attack came. I could see it all."

10–31 JANUARY, 1943, Guadalcanal
Some 50,000 U.S. troops attack the Japanese defenders. The Japanese are starving, and many are sick. The high command has therefore decided to leave Guadalcanal.

13 JANUARY Papua New Guinea
The Japanese lose control of the Kokoda Trail, a major route across the Owen Stanley mountains. This cuts off their access to Port Moresby, which they were planning to use as an air base.

18 JANUARY Poland
Jewish fighters in the Warsaw Ghetto begin attacking German troops.

2 FEBRUARY Soviet Union
The siege of Stalingrad ends when 93,000 German troops surrender. The Sixth Army has been unable to cope with the strain of food shortages and constant attacks.

14–22 FEBRUARY North Africa
The Battle of Kasserine Pass. Rommel's attack causes widespread panic among inexperienced U.S. troops. Rommel loses 2,000 men; the Americans 10,000.

16 FEBRUARY Germany
Students demonstrate against Hitler's regime in Munich. The protestors are led by brother and sister Hans and Sophie Scholl, leaders of the anti-Nazi White Rose student group at the University of Munich. They fail in their plan to start a revolt that will topple the government. The Scholls are arrested and executed on the 21st.

18 FEBRUARY Burma
Brigadier Orde Wingate launches the first British Chindit mission. A 3,000-strong force parachutes behind Japanese lines to begin raids on supply lines. However, the six-week mission is only partly successful.

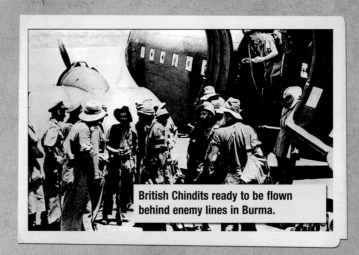

British Chindits ready to be flown behind enemy lines in Burma.

Chindit – a British soldier who fought behind Japanese lines in Burma.

2–5 MARCH Bismarck Sea

In the Battle of the Bismarck Sea, Allied warships sink eight Japanese transports and four destroyers. The Allies lose six aircraft and the Japanese 25.

14 MARCH Soviet Union

German forces under General Erich von Manstein destroy the Soviet Third Tank Army. The Soviets have now abandoned nearly 9,600 square km (6,000 sq miles) of newly-won ground in the face of Manstein's armoured attack. This has prevented a total Axis collapse on the Eastern Front.

15 MARCH Soviet Union

The Germans recapture Kharkov and Belgorod three days later. The victory encourages the Germans to launch Operation Citadel, a plan to destroy 500,000 Red Army troops around the city of Kursk.

12 APRIL Soviet Union

The Germans find a mass grave in Katyn Forest. It contains the bodies of 10,000

A Japanese merchant ship is attacked by U.S. aircraft in the Pacific.

Polish army officers executed by the Soviet secret police in 1939.

17 APRIL Germany

The U.S. Eighth Army Air Force attacks Bremen. Sixteen of the 115 B-17 Flying Fortress bombers are shot down.

13 MAY North Africa

Axis forces surrender to the Allies. Some 620,000 Axis casualties and prisoners have been lost in North Africa.

KEY PEOPLE: Franklin D. Roosevelt

Franklin D. Roosevelt (1882–1945) was U.S. president from 1933 to 1945. He turned the United States into an 'arsenal of democracy' to supply the Allies with weapons. When the United States entered the war in 1941, Roosevelt made the key decision to follow a 'Germany First' strategy. U.S. troops would concentrate on defeating Hitler rather than defeating Japan. Roosevelt died three weeks before the end of the war in Europe.

Strategy – a long-term plan of action.

EYEWITNESS: General Mellenthin, Kursk, 1943

"The entire area had been laid with mines; and the Russian defence along the whole line was supported by tanks operating with the advantages of high ground. Our assault troops suffered considerable casualties, and 3 Panzer Division had to beat off counter-attacks. In spite of several massive bombing attacks by the Luftwaffe, the Russian defensive fire did not decrease to any extent."

10 JUNE Germany
Operation Pointblank is launched. This series of attacks on Germany by British and U.S. bomber forces will last until the Allies invade France in June 1944. U.S. strategy concentrates on daylight precision raids to destroy Germany's air forces and its aircraft industry. British attacks focus on night-time saturation bombing to undermine Germany's economy and civilian morale.

5 JULY Soviet Union
The Battle of Kursk. More than 6,000 German and Soviet tanks and assault guns take part in the war's largest armoured battle. The Germans make little progress against Soviet antitank defences.

9 JULY Sicily
U.S. and British troops invade the island.

16–17 MAY Germany
Dams on the Möhne and Eder rivers are smashed by British Lancaster bombers using specially-designed 'bouncing bombs'. The raid badly disrupts power and water supplies to the Ruhr, one of Germany's most important industrial regions. The British lose eight aircraft in the attack, but it is a great morale boost.

16 MAY Poland
The Warsaw Ghetto uprising ends. It has been brutally crushed by the Germans, who have used flamethrowers to burn out Jewish fighters. A total of around 14,000 Jews have been killed. Another 22,000 are sent to concentration camps, and 20,000 to labour camps.

12–13 JULY Soviet Union
At Kursk, the Soviets launch a counter-attack around the village of Prokhorovka. In the tank battle that follows, the Germans are defeated. During the whole battle, they have lost more than 550 tanks and 500,000 men killed, wounded or missing.

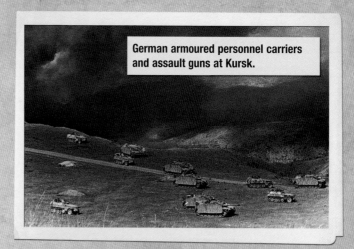

German armoured personnel carriers and assault guns at Kursk.

Counter-attack – an attack by a defending force.

The results of the British bombing raid on the city of Hamburg.

24 JULY–2 AUGUST Germany

A series of massive British bombing raids on Hamburg leave about 50,000 people dead and 800,000 homeless.

25 JULY Italy

The king of Italy sacks Benito Mussolini, who is arrested. Marshal Pietro Badoglio forms a new government. Badoglio hopes that the Allies will quickly occupy most of Italy before it falls under German control.

17 AUGUST Sicily

The capture of Messina marks the Allied victory on Sicily. About 10,000 Germans have been killed or captured. The Italians have lost 132,000 men, mainly as prisoners. Sicily is now a springboard for an invasion of Italy.

22–23 AUGUST Soviet Union

Kharkov is retaken by the Red Army. The Soviets now threaten the Ukraine.

9 SEPTEMBER Italy

Lieutenant General Mark Clark's U.S. Fifth Army lands in southern Italy with the British X Corps.

12 SEPTEMBER Italy

German airborne troops led by Lieutenant Colonel Otto Skorzeny rescue Mussolini from imprisonment in Gran Sasso.

25 SEPTEMBER Soviet Union

The Soviets recapture Smolensk. Germany's Army Group Centre is now falling back.

12–22 OCTOBER Italy

U.S. forces make slow progress north in the face of bad weather. The British Eighth

EYEWITNESS: Robert Sherrod, Tarawa Atoll, November 1943

"We jumped into the little tractor boat and quickly settled on the deck. 'Oh God, I'm scared,' said the little Marine, a telephone operator, who sat next to me forward in the boat. I gritted my teeth and tried to force a smile that would not come and tried to stop quivering all over (now I was shaking from fear). I said, in an effort to be reassuring, 'I'm scared, too'. I never made a more truthful statement in my life."

Corps – a military unit made up of several divisions.

34

TURNING POINTS: Resistance

In countries overrun by the Germans and Japanese, some people were determined to oppose the occupiers. Resistance involved demonstrations, strikes, gathering intelligence, helping escaped Allied prisoners of war and sabotage. The dangers of fighting back against occupiers were great. Many captured Resistance fighters were tortured and killed. Resistance groups in Europe and East Asia helped the Allied victory — but in most cases they only came out into the open after the war (right).

Army also advances north. The Germans have created strong defences in central Italy, known as the Gustav Line.

25 OCTOBER Burma
The Burma to Siam rail link is completed. It has been built by the Japanese using Allied prisoners and local people as labour. About 12,000 prisoners have died as a result of accidents, abuse, disease and starvation.

6 NOVEMBER Soviet Union
The Soviets take Kiev. The victory traps the German Seventeenth Army in the Crimea.

20 NOVEMBER Gilbert Islands
Some 18,600 U.S. Marines land on Tarawa and Betio. More than 1,000 Marines are killed in fierce fighting before the islands are captured on the 23rd.

28 NOVEMBER Iran
In Tehran, British Prime Minister Winston Churchill meets U.S. President Franklin D. Roosevelt and Soviet leader Joseph Stalin. They give priority to a cross-Channel invasion of German-occupied Europe and a landing in southern France in May 1944.

26 DECEMBER Arctic Ocean
The Battle of the North Cape. British warships sink the German battleship *Scharnhorst*. Some 1,800 Germans drown.

Soviet Red Army troops and artillery in action on the outskirts of Kiev.

Sabotage – destruction of an enemy's property.

14–17 JANUARY, 1944, Soviet Union

Red Army attacks on the German forces besieging Leningrad result in heavy fighting and a German retreat. Some 830,000 civilians have died during the three-year-long siege.

22 JANUARY Italy

The Allies attempt to overcome the Gustav Line by landing troops behind it at Anzio, on Italy's western coast. Commanded by U.S. General John Lucas, the initial attack meets virtually no resistance. The road to Rome is open – but Lucas orders his forces to dig in and create defensive positions.

30 JANUARY Marshall Islands

The Americans begin a planned conquest of the Marshall Islands that aims to attack Japanese-held islands and Japanese air bases. Operation Flintlock begins with an amphibious assault on an undefended island in Majuro Atoll.

American dive-bombers return from attacking Japanese ships.

1–4 FEBRUARY Marshall Islands

American forces launch an amphibious assault against Kwajalein Atoll. Some 40,000 U.S. Marines and infantry land on the islands of Roi, Namur and Kwajalein. Total Japanese losses are 11,612 men killed. The Americans lose more than 1,000.

4–24 FEBRUARY Burma

The Japanese launch Operation Ha-Go to force the Allies back to the Indian border.

TURNING POINTS: Women at war

Women on the home front did not only have to complete their usual daily chores. With men away fighting, many also had to go to work to support the war effort. Women in Germany became workers and, later in the war, fighters (right). In the Soviet Union, women fought in the army or flew warplanes. In America and Britain, women worked in factories producing weapons and aircraft. For many women, this was their first employment. After the war, many chose not to go back to being housewives.

Amphibious assault – an attack by soldiers who land from the sea.

EYEWITNESS: Leon Degrelle, SS comander, Russia, 1944

"Snow fell endlessly in the evening. It was soon a foot high. Twenty or thirty thousand people waited in our village for some kind of military end to the drama, with no accommodation. Oblivious to the danger, the people stood out in the open in groups around fires they had lit in the snow. Lying out in this biting cold would have meant certain death."

Initial Japanese attacks are successful, but Allied troops then fight back.

18–22 FEBRUARY Marshall Islands
U.S. forces complete their conquest of the islands with the seizure of Eniwetok Atoll. The Japanese lose 3,400 men.

7–8 MARCH India/Burma
Operation U-Go begins; the Japanese assault aims to drive the Allies back into India by attacking their bases at Imphal and Kohima.

20–22 MARCH Italy
Allied attacks fail to overcome Monte Cassino, part of the Gustav Line.

9 MAY Soviet Union
The Red Army liberates the Black Sea port of Sevastopol. It is a crushing defeat for the German defenders, who have lost 100,000 men killed and captured.

11–18 MAY Italy
The Allies break through the Gustav Line near Monte Cassino. On the 17th, the Germans evacuate the monastery at Monte Cassino to avoid becoming surrounded. Next day, the Polish 12th Podolski Regiment storms the ruined buildings.

3 JUNE India
The 64-day Battle of Kohima ends with a Japanese withdrawal. The fighting has been some of the most savage of the whole war. In the end, however, it is a lack of supplies that forces the Japanese to fall back, rather than British and Indian attacks.

3–5 JUNE Italy
The Germans abandon Rome. U.S. troops enter the city on the 5th. It is the first Axis capital to be captured.

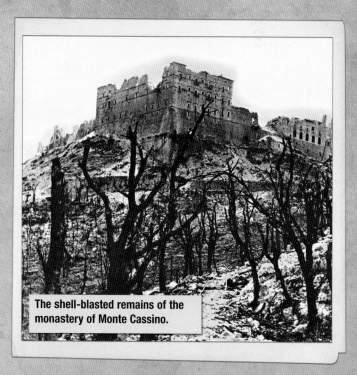

The shell-blasted remains of the monastery of Monte Cassino.

Marine – a soldier based on a ship who fights on land.

TURNING POINTS: Kamikaze

Kamikaze is Japanese for 'Divine Wind'. It was a suicide tactic used by the Japanese to destroy U.S. shipping by crashing explosive-filled aircraft into vessels. The tactic was first used in the Battle of Leyte Gulf in October 1944. Kamikaze pilots tried to hit the deck of their target to cause maximum damage (against carriers, they aimed for the central elevator, seen right). During the Okinawa battles in 1945, Japanese pilots flew 1,900 suicide missions.

6 JUNE France

D-Day. The Allied invasion of Normandy, codenamed Operation Overlord, begins. Paratroopers land to seize key inland targets and seaborne forces storm five beaches. By the end of the day, the Allies have a toehold in Europe at a cost of 2,500 dead.

10 JUNE France

German soldiers kill 642 civilians in the town of Oradour-sur-Glane. The atrocity is a retaliation for attacks on a German SS Panzer division by the French Resistance.

13 JUNE France

A Tiger tank commanded by Lieutenant Michael Wittmann destroys 27 British tanks and armoured vehicles in a battle at the village of Villers-Bocage, Normandy.

19–21 JUNE Philippine Sea

The Battle of the Philippine Sea. The Japanese Combined Fleet is defeated by the U.S. 5th Fleet. It loses three aircraft carriers and 460 combat aircraft and pilots in what U.S. pilots name the 'Great Marianas Turkey Shoot'.

22 JUNE Soviet Union

The Red Army launches Operation Bagration against German Army Group Centre. The Soviets enjoy a four-to-one superiority in tanks and aircraft.

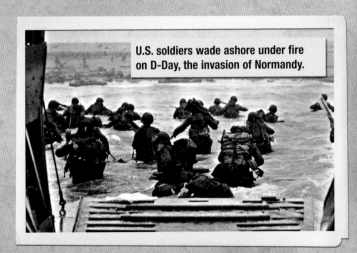

U.S. soldiers wade ashore under fire on D-Day, the invasion of Normandy.

Retaliation – revenge for a previous event.

30 JUNE Britain
To date, 2,000 German V1 'Flying Bombs' have been launched against England, mostly against London.

9 JULY Saipan
U.S. troops secure the island. At least 8,000 Japanese troops and civilians have committed suicide rather than surrender to the Americans.

20 JULY Germany
German officers try to kill Adolf Hitler. Count Schenk von Stauffenberg plants a bomb in a conference room, but fails to kill Hitler. The failure of the plot results in the arrest, torture and execution of dozens of suspects.

1 AUGUST Poland
The Warsaw uprising – 38,000 soldiers of the Polish Home Army fight the Germans.

10 AUGUST Marianas Islands
Japanese resistance on Guam finally ends after fierce fighting. However, the last

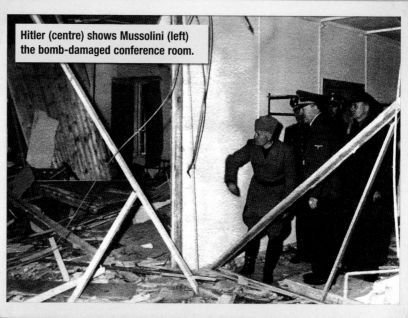

Hitler (centre) shows Mussolini (left) the bomb-damaged conference room.

Japanese soldier on the island does not give himself up until 1960.

25 AUGUST France
General Dietrich von Choltitz, commander of the German garrison of Paris, surrenders the city to the Allies.

2 SEPTEMBER Finland
Finland, exhausted by the war, accepts a peace treaty with the Soviet Union. The Finns cut relations with Germany.

EYEWITNESS: Jim Irving, U.S. Army, Omaha Beach, 6 June, 1944

"Our main objective was to clear eight lanes for landing craft on the two beaches. This was impossible as the infantry and tank battalion landing in front of us were pinned down at the water's edge. At 0900 the beach master stopped additional vehicles due to congestion on the beach. Only engineers and infantry were allowed to be incoming on Omaha Beach until, at 11 am, with all troops on shore we cleared the beach."

Uprising – a revolt against a ruler.

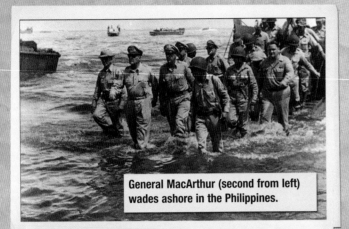

General MacArthur (second from left) wades ashore in the Philippines.

2 OCTOBER Poland

After a two-month battle, the last Poles in Warsaw surrender to the Germans. Polish deaths number 150,000.

20 OCTOBER Philippines

As the U.S. Sixth Army lands on Leyte Island, General Douglas MacArthur wades ashore. He keeps a promise he made two years earlier: "I shall return."

23–26 OCTOBER Philippines

The Japanese Combined Fleet is defeated at the Battle of Leyte Gulf. It loses 500 aircraft, 28 ships and a submarine. U.S. losses are 200 aircraft and six ships.

17 SEPTEMBER Holland

Operation Market Garden, an Allied attack on occupied Holland, begins. Paratroopers land near Arnhem, Eindhoven and Nijmegen to seize key bridges. But the Germans are waiting.The Allies suffer heavy casualties.

22–25 SEPTEMBER Holland

The paratroopers retreat from Arnhem. The British alone have lost 2,500 dead.

16 DECEMBER Belgium

Hitler begins Operation Watch on the Rhine, which aims to capture Antwerp in Belgium. The Germans attack in thick fog. At first they advance, but U.S. paratroopers hold out in Bastogne.

TURNING POINTS: The Holocaust

The Holocaust was the Nazi plan to exterminate Europe's Jews and other 'undesirables'. The Nazis saw the Jews as the enemy of 'Aryan' Germans. They sent Jews from occupied countries to concentration camps, where they were used as slave labour. In extermination camps, hundreds of thousands of people died in gas chambers. The six million victims included not just Jews (right) but Roma (gypsies), homosexuals and the Nazis' political opponents.

Destroyer – a small, fast warship.

EYEWITNESS: James Fahey, U.S. Navy, October 1944

"It was quite a sight. Japanese planes were coming at us from all directions. Before the attack started we did not know that they were suicide planes, with no intention of returning to their base. They had one thing in mind and that was to crash into our ships, bombs and all. You have to blow them up; to damage them doesn't mean much."

9 JANUARY, 1945, Philippines
Units of the U.S. Sixth Army make unopposed landings on the island of Luzon.

12–17 JANUARY Poland
The Red Army begins its Vistula–Oder Offensive against the Germans. Soviet forces totalling more than two million men make rapid advances along the whole front.

27 JANUARY Poland
The Red Army liberates the Nazi death camp at Auschwitz. The SS had evacuated the camp nine days previously, leaving behind a few hundred sick inmates in the camp's hospital block.

28 JANUARY Belgium
The Ardennes Offensive has cost the Germans 100,000 killed, wounded and captured. The Americans have lost 81,000 killed, wounded or captured. The Germans have also lost 800 tanks.

30 JANUARY Germany
Soviet forces reach the River Oder, only 160 km (100 miles) from Berlin. The Red Army has advanced 568 km (355 miles) and liberated all of Poland and a large part of Czechoslovakia. Its offensive has inflicted losses on the Germans of 500,000 dead, wounded or captured.

3 FEBRUARY Philippines
U.S. forces begin an attack on the capital, Manila, which is defended by 17,000 Japanese troops. The Japanese garrison destroys the city in the 'Rape of Manila'; after a month's fighting, it is wiped out.

4 FEBRUARY Soviet Union
Joseph Stalin, President Franklin D. Roosevelt and Prime Minister Winston Churchill meet at Yalta in the Crimea to discuss postwar Europe. The 'Big Three' decide that Germany will be divided into four zones, administered by Britain, France, the United States and the Soviet Union.

Churchill (left), Roosevelt (centre) and Stalin (right) at the Yalta Conference.

Liberate – to set free.

KEY WEAPONS: The Atomic Bomb

The atomic bomb used the energy released by splitting atoms to start a chain reaction that produced a huge explosion. The secret American programme to make the bomb, codenamed the Manhattan Project, began in December 1941 at Los Alamos in New Mexico. It involved over 60,000 workers, led by J. Robert Oppenheimer. The new weapon had the destructive power of a raid by 2,000 B-29 bombers. The first bomb was successfully tested in New Mexico on 16 July, 1945.

13–14 FEBRUARY Germany

Some 805 British bombers attack Dresden. At least 50,000 people are killed. The next morning, the city is bombed again by 400 aircraft of the U.S. Eighth Army Air Force.

14 FEBRUARY Germany

As a result of the Red Army's advance, half of the 2.3 million population of German East Prussia flee west. Thousands of civilians die from cold or exhaustion.

17 FEBRUARY Iwo Jima

Under the command of Lieutenant General Holland M. Smith, U.S. Marines land on the island of Iwo Jima. The attackers are pinned down by heavy artillery and small-arms fire from the 21,000-man Japanese garrison.

23 FEBRUARY Iwo Jima

U.S. Marines raise the Stars and Stripes flag on the summit of Mount Suribachi. Fighting continues on the island, however.

7 MARCH Japan

A U.S. bombing raid on Tokyo sets alight over 25.6 square kilometres (16 sq miles) of the city and kills 100,000 people.

16 MARCH Iwo Jima

The Americans declare the island secure. They have lost 6,821 soldiers and sailors. Of the 21,000 Japanese defenders, nearly 20,000 are dead.

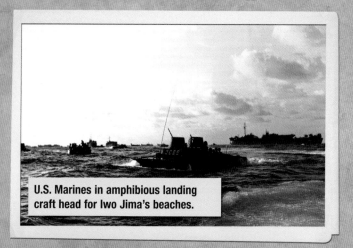

U.S. Marines in amphibious landing craft head for Iwo Jima's beaches.

Garrison – a military post.

EYEWITNESS: Dorothea von Schwanenfluegel, Berlin, April 1945

"The Soviets battled the German soldiers and drafted civilians street by street until we could hear explosions and rifle fire right in our immediate vicinity. Shots shattered our windows and shells exploded in our garden, and suddenly the Soviets were on our street. Shaken by the battle around us and numb with fear, we watched from behind the small cellar windows facing the street as the tanks and an endless convoy of troops rolled by."

23 MARCH Germany
Field Marshal Bernard Montgomery's British forces begin crossing the River Rhine on the German border. Next day, U.S. troops begin crossing the river. German units offer little resistance.

1 APRIL Okinawa
Operation Iceberg. The U.S. Tenth Army, with 183,000 men, lands on the island, which is only 520 kilometres (325 miles) from Japan. The island's airfields and harbours will be used for the proposed invasion of the Japanese mainland. Japan has 80,000 defenders on the island.

7 APRIL Pacific Ocean
The *Yamato*, the world's largest battleship, is sunk by U.S. warplanes on its way to fight at Okinawa.

9 APRIL Italy
The final campaign in Italy begins as the U.S. Fifth and British Eighth Armies attack German Army Group Centre.

12 APRIL United States
President Franklin D. Roosevelt dies of a brain haemorrhage in Warm Springs, Georgia. Vice President Harry S. Truman takes over as president.

16 APRIL Germany
The Soviets attack Berlin. The Red Army has 2.5 million men, 41,600 guns, 6,250 tanks and 7,500 combat aircraft. The German defenders have one million men, 10,400 guns, 1,500 tanks and 3,300 aircraft.

U.S. forces land on the island of Okinawa in early April 1945.

Haemorrhage – the bursting of a blood vessel.

TURNING POINTS: Casualties of War

No war in history cost as many lives as World War II. The Soviet Union lost more citizens than the other nations put together: 7.5 million military dead plus 15 million civilian deaths. Germany lost 2.8 million military dead and 500,000 civilians. Japan's total was 1.5 million military dead, plus 300,000 civilians who died in U.S. bombing raids. Other nations lost far fewer lives: the United States 292,000; Great Britain 397,762; France 210,600; and Italy 117,000. In all, civilian war deaths numbered 34 million.

25 APRIL Germany

Berlin is surrounded by the Red Army. By the 27th, 'Fortress Berlin' has been reduced to an east-to-west belt 16 km (10 miles) long by 5 km (3 miles) wide. Soviet rockets and bombs kill many defenders.

28 APRIL Italy

Mussolini, trying to flee to Austria with his girlfriend Claretta Petacci, is captured by communist partisans. They are both shot.

29 APRIL Italy

After a secret deal with the Americans, General Heinrich von Vietinghoff, German commander-in-chief in Italy, surrenders his forces to the Allies.

30 APRIL Germany

Adolf Hitler and his wife Eva Braun commit suicide in Berlin. Hitler shoots himself, while Braun takes poison. Their bodies are later burned by the SS.

2 MAY Germany

Following a savage three-day battle, the Reichstag in Berlin falls to the Red Army. Taking the city has cost the Soviets 300,000 men killed, wounded or missing. The Germans have lost one million men.

3 MAY Burma

After 38 months of Japanese occupation, Rangoon falls to the Allies without a fight.

Red Army troops fly the Soviet flag over the ruins of Berlin.

Reichstag – the German parliament.

The Japanese city of Hiroshima after it was devastated by an atomic bomb.

8 MAY Europe
Victory in Europe (VE) Day. The Allies formally accept the German surrender.

22 JUNE Okinawa
Japanese resistance on the island ends. The battle has cost the Japanese 110,000 dead. U.S. Navy losses amount to 9,731, of whom 4,907 are killed, while the Tenth Army has suffered 7,613 men killed or missing and 31,807 wounded.

17 JULY–2 AUGUST Germany
U.S. President Harry Truman, Soviet leader Joseph Stalin and new British Prime Minister Clement Attlee meet at Potsdam to discuss post-war policy. Japan is informed that further resistance will lead to the 'utter devastation of the Japanese homeland'.

6 AUGUST Japan
The B-29 Superfortress *Enola Gay* drops an atomic bomb on the Japanese city of Hiroshima, killing 70,000 and injuring the same number.

9 AUGUST Manchuria
A Soviet offensive by 1.5 million men begins against the Japanese Kwantung Army.

9 AUGUST Japan
An atomic bomb is dropped on Nagasaki. The bomb kills 35,000 people and injures 60,000. The Japanese decide to surrender.

15 AUGUST Japan
Victory over Japan (VJ) Day. The Japanese surrender is announced.

23 AUGUST Manchuria
The campaign in Manchuria ends in total Soviet victory. The Japanese have lost over 80,000 men. Soviet losses are 8,000 men killed and 22,000 wounded.

2 SEPTEMBER Japan
Aboard the battleship *Missouri* in Tokyo Bay, Japanese officials sign the Instrument of Surrender. World War II is finally over.

EYEWITNESS: Dr. Michihiko Hachiya, Hiroshima, 1945

"Suddenly, a strong flash of light startled me — and then another. So well does one recall little things that I remember vividly how a stone lantern in the garden became brilliantly lit and I debated whether this light was caused by a magnesium flare or sparks from a passing trolley. All over the right side of my body I was cut and bleeding."

Manchuria – a region of northeast China.

Glossary

amphibious assault: an attack by soldiers who land from the sea

appeasement: avoiding conflict by giving in to someone's demands

'buffer state': a country between two enemy states

Chindit: a British soldier who fought behind Japanese lines in Burma

civil war: a war between two opposing groups of citizens of the same country

commandos: special forces soldiers

convoy: a number of ships or vehicles travelling together

corps: a military unit made up of several divisions

counter-attack: an attack by a defending force

destroyer: a small, fast warship

division: an army unit made up of 15,000 to 20,000 soldiers

evacuation: the removal of people from a dangerous area

expeditionary force: an army sent to serve abroad

extermination: the murder of an entire people

fascist: a supporter of a strongly nationalistic and militaristic political party

garrison: a military post

ghetto: part of a city where Jews were forced to live

haemorrhage: the bursting of a blood vessel

liberate: to set free

Manchuria: a region of northeast China

marine: a soldier based on a ship who fights on land

morale: the emotional well-being of people

occupation: military control of part of a country by forces from another

panzer: German word for a tank

paratrooper: a soldier who jumps from an aircraft with a parachute

partisan: a soldier who fights behind enemy lines

pocket battleship: a powerful warship smaller than a battleship

rebel: someone who fights against a government or leader

Reichstag: the German parliament

reservists: part of an army called on to fight in an emergency

retaliation: revenge for a previous event

sabotage: destruction of an enemy's property

strategic: something that is useful in achieving a long-term goal

strategy: a long-term plan of action

surrender: to stop fighting and give in to the enemy

U-boat: a German submarine

ultimatum: a demand made by one country on another

uprising: a revolt against a ruler

warlord: a military commander who has political power over a region

'Wolf Pack': a group of 15 to 20 German U-boats

Further resources

BOOKS ABOUT WORLD WAR II

World War II (DK Eyewitness Books) by Simon Adams, DK Children, 2007

Key Battles of World War II (20th Century Perspectives) by Fiona Reynoldson, Heinemann, 2001

My Second World War (My War) by Daniel James, Franklin Watts, 2008

Second World War by Dennis Hamley, Franklin Watts, 2007

Timelines: World War II by Nathaniel Harris, Franklin Watts, 2007

The Second World War (How Did it Happen?) by Cath Senker, Franklin Watts, 2007

World War Two: Causes and Consequences by Simon Adams, Franklin Watts, 2005

USEFUL WEBSITES

www.worldwar-2.net/

www.euronet.nl/users/wilfried/ww2/ww2.htm

www.spartacus.schoolnet.co.uk/2WW.htm

www.eyewitnesstohistory.com/w2frm.htm

www.ibiblio.org/hyperwar/

www.teacheroz.com/wwii.htm

Index

Afrika Korps 21
aircraft carriers 12, 24, 27, 28, 29, 38
appeasement 10, 34
Atlantic War 11, 12, 14, 18, 19, 21, 23, 24, 26
atomic bomb 42, 45
Auschwitz 24, 41

Barbarossa, Operation 23
Battle of Britain 18
Bismarck 23
Blitz 19, 22
Blitzkrieg 15
British Expeditionary Force 12
Burma 31, 35, 36, 37, 44

Chamberlain, Neville 9, 10
Churchill, Winston 6, 16, 35, 41
concentration camps 24, 33, 40
Condor Legion 9
convoys 18, 19, 21, 26

D-Day 38
Doolittle Raid 27

'Final Solution' 23

Gandhi, Mahatma 6
George, Lloyd 6
Graf Spee 14

Heydrich, Reinhard 23, 26
Hitler, Adolf 5, 8, 9, 10, 12, 13, 26, 31, 39, 40, 44
Holocaust 23, 40

Italy 20, 25, 34, 35, 36, 37, 43, 44

Jews 5, 10, 12, 23, 24, 26, 29, 33, 40

kamikaze 38, 40
Kiev 7

Kursk, Battle of 33
League of Nations 5, 14
Lend-Lease Act 21, 22

MacArthur, General Douglas 40
Mannerheim, Field Marshal Karl von 14
Monte Cassino 37
Montgomery, Field Marshal Bernard 43
Mussolini, Benito 5, 7, 8, 9, 17, 20, 34, 44

Nanking 8
Nazi Party 5, 8, 12
North Africa 20, 21, 23, 24, 28, 29, 30, 31, 32

Pacific War 7, 22, 23, 25, 27, 28, 29, 42
Pearl Harbor 24, 25
Philippines 27, 40, 41
Poland 4, 5, 7, 11, 12, 13, 24, 29, 31, 33, 39, 40, 41
'Polish Corridor' 5

resistance movements 35, 38
Rommel, Erwin 17, 21, 28, 29, 30, 31
Roosevelt, Franklin D. 16, 20, 21, 32, 35, 41

Sealion, Operation 19
Sicily 33, 34
Stalin, Joseph 26, 28, 35, 41

Taranto, Battle of 20
Typhoon, Operation 24

U-boats 12, 14, 18, 19, 24, 26

Versailles Treaty 4, 5, 6, 7
Vichy France 17

Warsaw Ghetto 29, 31, 33
'Wolf Pack' 19